AF270653

Animal Fun Facts
FUN FACTS ABOUT
MONKEYS
by Julie Murray
Dash!
LEVELED READERS
2
An Imprint of Abdo Zoom • abdobooks.com

Level 1 – Beginning
Short and simple sentences with familiar words or patterns for children who are beginning to understand how letters and sounds go together.

Level 2 – Emerging
Longer words and sentences with more complex language patterns for readers who are practicing common words and letter sounds.

Level 3 – Transitional
More developed language and vocabulary for readers who are becoming more independent.

abdobooks.com

Published by Abdo Zoom, a division of ABDO, PO Box 398166, Minneapolis, Minnesota 55439. Copyright © 2022 by Abdo Consulting Group, Inc. International copyrights reserved in all countries. No part of this book may be reproduced in any form without written permission from the publisher. Dash!™ is a trademark and logo of Abdo Zoom.

Printed in the United States of America, North Mankato, Minnesota.
052021
092021

Photo Credits: Alamy, iStock, Minden Pictures, Shutterstock
Production Contributors: Kenny Abdo, Jennie Forsberg, Grace Hansen, John Hansen
Design Contributors: Candice Keimig, Neil Klinepier

Library of Congress Control Number: 2020919487

Publisher's Cataloging in Publication Data

Names: Murray, Julie, author.
Title: Fun facts about monkeys / by Julie Murray
Description: Minneapolis, Minnesota : Abdo Zoom, 2022 | Series: Animal fun facts | Includes online resources and index.
Identifiers: ISBN 9781098224479 (lib. bdg.) | ISBN 9781098225414 (ebook) | ISBN 9781098225889 (Read-to-Me ebook)
Subjects: LCSH: Monkeys--Juvenile literature. | Monkeys--Behavior--Juvenile literature. | Primates--Behavior--Juvenile literature. | Questions and answers--Juvenile literature. | Animal behavior--Juvenile literature.
Classification: DDC 599.8--dc23

Table of Contents

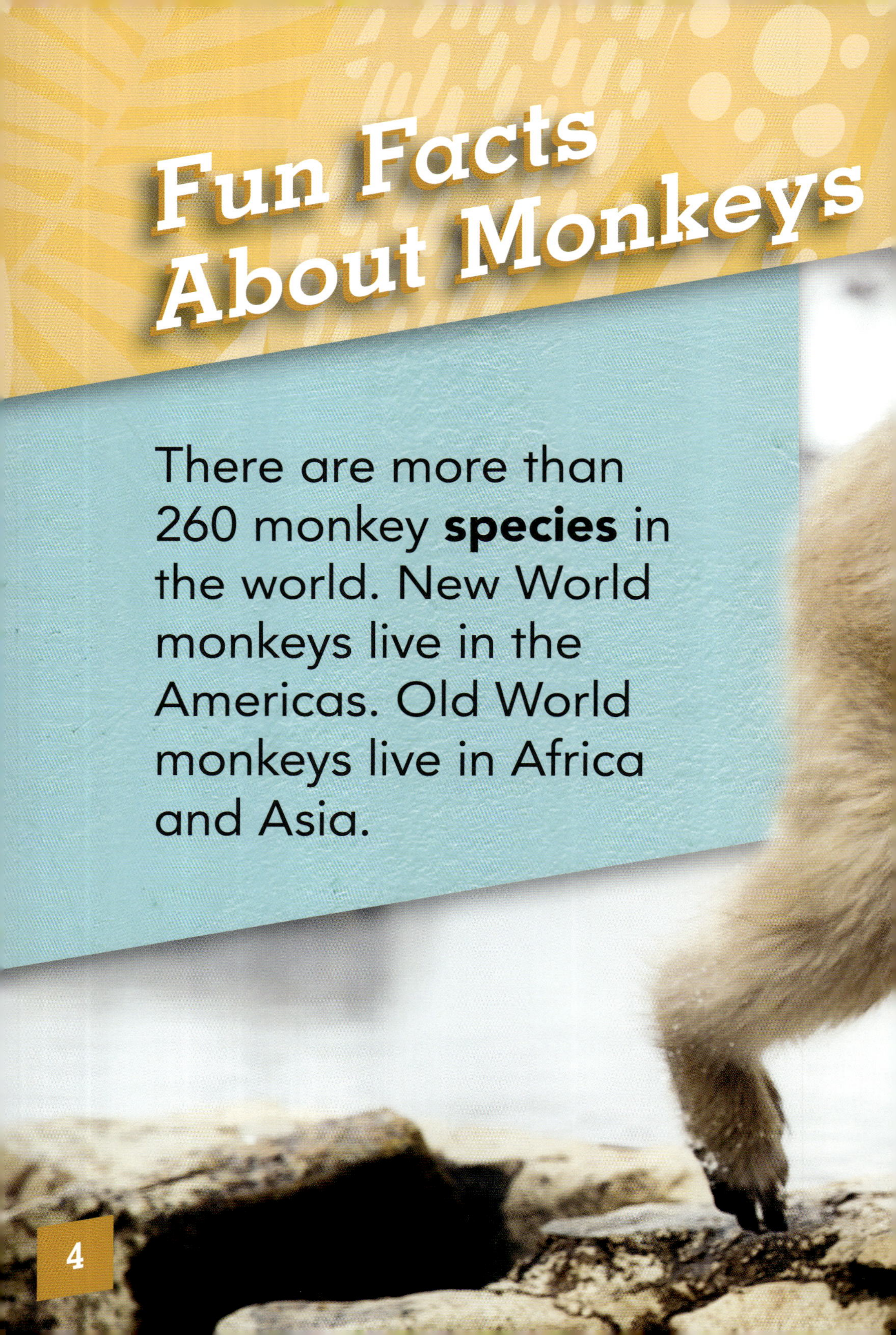

Fun Facts About Monkeys

There are more than 260 monkey **species** in the world. New World monkeys live in the Americas. Old World monkeys live in Africa and Asia.

Monkeys are smart! Some can even solve math problems. Capuchins are the smartest. They have been using tools for more than 3,000 years.

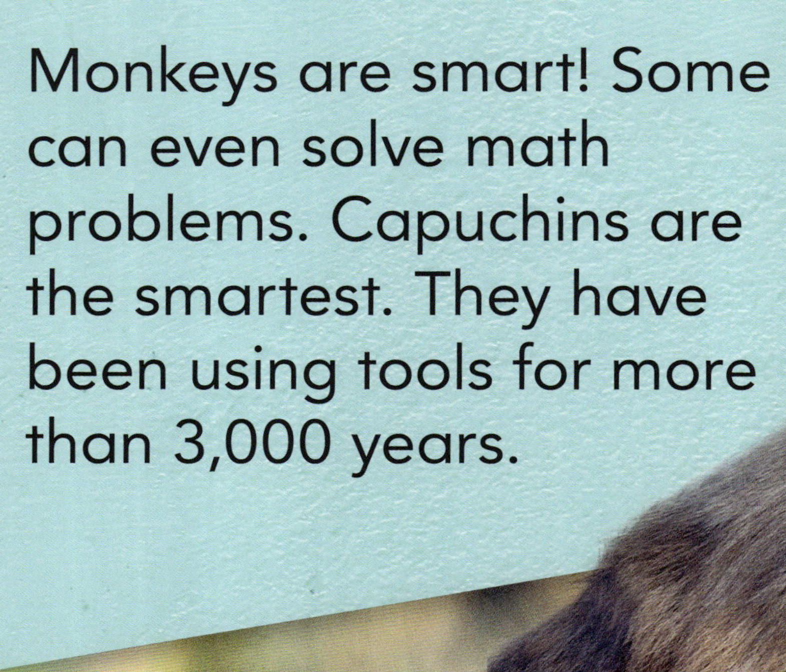

Rhesus **macaques** are very smart, but naughty. They have been known to find food in towns and make a special call to the rest of the group. Then they have a feast!

The howler monkey is loud!
It is one of the loudest
animals in the world. Its
call can be heard 3 miles
(4.8 km) away.

11

Squirrel monkeys urinate on their hands and feet! They do this to mark their territory. As they climb through trees, their scent is left behind.

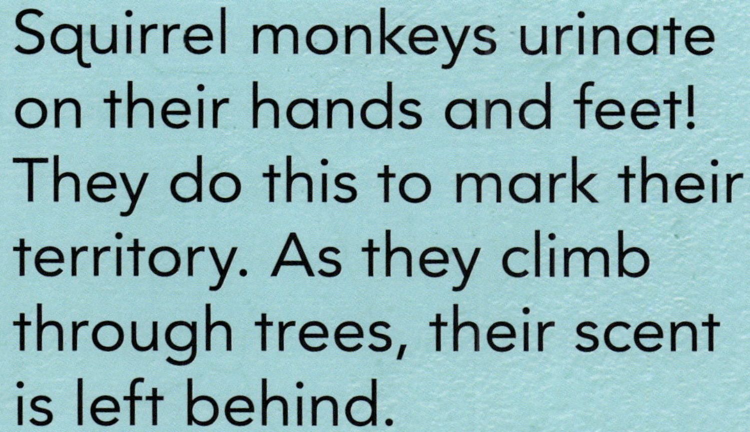

Spider monkeys have long tails. The tail can be 3 feet (1 m) long. Spider monkeys can hold, carry, and catch things with their tails!

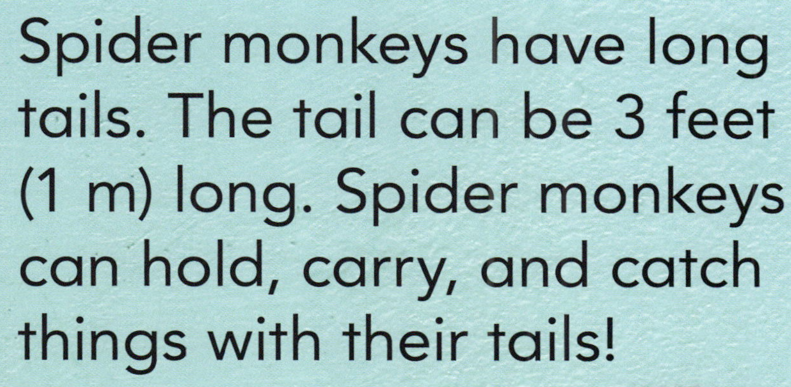

The patas monkey is fast. It can move 34 miles per hour (55 km/h). It is the fastest **primate** on Earth!

The pygmy marmoset
is the smallest monkey
species. It is just 5 inches
(13 cm) tall. It can fit in
your hand!

The mandrill is the largest monkey. It can be 3 feet (1 m) tall and weigh up to 80 pounds (36.3 kg). It is one of the most brightly colored mammals.

Proboscis Monkey

Size: Up to 2.5 feet (0.8 m) tall; Up to 50 pounds (22.7 kg) (males)

Appearance: light brown fur that turns red at the head and shoulders; males grow very large noses that can make noise

Range: Borneo, an island country in Southeast Asia

Habitat: jungles near rivers, coastal mangroves, and swamps

Diet: fruit, seeds, leaves

Lifespan: 20 years

Glossary

macaques – any of a family of monkeys of the East Indies, Asia, and Africa that have cheek pouches and tails that do not grasp objects.

primate – any animal in the category of mammals that includes humans, monkeys, apes, and some other animals. Most primates have large brains and flexible hands.

species – a group of living things that look alike, share a common name, and can have young with one another.

Index

Online Resources

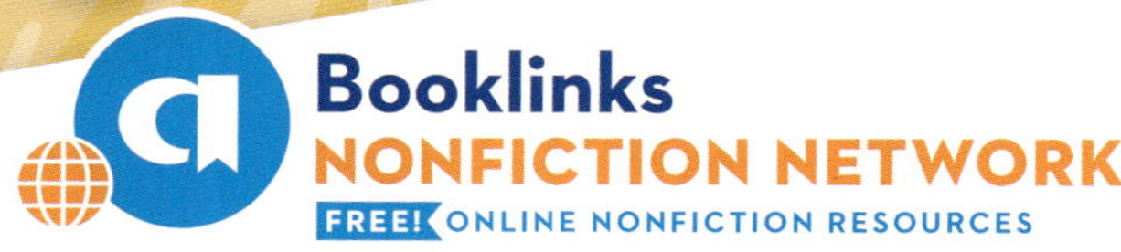

To learn more about monkeys, please visit **abdobooklinks.com** or scan this QR code. These links are routinely monitored and updated to provide the most current information available.